THE WATER CYCLE AT WORK

By George Pendergast

Gareth Stevens
PUBLISHING

Please visit our website, www.garethstevens.com. For a free color catalog of all our high-quality books, call toll free 1-800-542-2595 or fax 1-877-542-2596.

Library of Congress Cataloging-in-Publication Data

Pendergast, George.
The water cycle at work / by George Pendergast.
p. cm. — (Cycles in nature)
Includes index.
ISBN 978-1-4824-1671-8 (pbk.)
ISBN 978-1-4824-1672-5 (6-pack)
ISBN 978-1-4824-1670-1 (library binding)
1. Water — Juvenile literature. 2. Hydrologic cycle — Juvenile literature. I. Pendergast, George. II. Title.
GB662.3 P46 2015
551.48—d23

Published in 2016 by
Gareth Stevens Publishing
111 East 14th Street, Suite 349
New York, NY 10003

Designer: Sarah Liddell
Editor: Ryan Nagelhout

Photo credits: Cover, p. 1 mythja/Shutterstock.com; p. 5 Dudarev Mikhail/Shutterstock.com; p. 7 BMJ/Shutterstock.com; p. 9 leonello calvetti/Shutterstock.com; p. 11 Stefan Verheij/Shutterstock.com; p. 13 Phil Emmerson/Shutterstock.com; p. 15 (rain) andreiuc88/Shutterstock.com; p. 15 (snow) Volodymyr Burdiak/Shutterstock.com; p. 15 (hail) Andrzej Sliwinski/Shutterstock.com; p. 17 (salt water) EpicStockMedia/Shutterstock.com; p. 17 (freshwater) Mykola Mazuryk/Shutterstock.com; p. 17 (groundwater) Lightspring/Shutterstock.com; p. 19 Merkushev Vasiliy/Shutterstock.com; p. 21 FamVeld/Shutterstock.com.

Printed in the United States of America

CPSIA compliance information: Batch #CS16GS: For further information contact Gareth Stevens, New York, New York at 1-800-542-2595.

CONTENTS

Boldface words appear in the glossary.

Water Questions

Have you ever wondered how clouds are made? Or where all that water goes when it rains? When you get a glass of water, where did it come from? To get the answers to these questions, you need to understand the water cycle.

The water cycle is the movement of water on Earth and in the **atmosphere**. Water is traveling all the time! It can go deep underground and high up into the air. Many different forces help move water from place to place.

Collecting Water

Water **collects** in different places on Earth. More than 96 percent of water is salt water found in the oceans. Only 2.5 percent of Earth's water is freshwater found in rivers, lakes, and underground.

When water on Earth heats up, it becomes steam, or water vapor. This change is called evaporation. Warmth from the sun often causes evaporation. The warm water vapor in the air moves high into the sky.

sun

water vapor

water

11

Way Up High

Water vapor gets colder the higher it goes into the air. It starts to become liquid again. This is called condensation. The water collects and forms clouds. Wind moves clouds around as more water collects to make them bigger.

When too much water condenses and clouds get too heavy, the water falls back to Earth. This is called precipitation. Precipitation comes in many forms. It can be rain, snow, hail, or any mix of these.

rain

snow

hail

15

Down It Goes

When precipitation falls, it often lands back on Earth's **surface**. Precipitation can collect in the oceans to become salt water or in lakes as freshwater. **Gravity** can also pull water down into the ground, where it becomes groundwater.

salt water

freshwater

groundwater

Plants **absorb** some groundwater, but most goes through rock and soil and reaches the water table. The water table is the point in the ground where water completely fills in the parts between rock and soil. This is called the zone of **saturation**.

The Water Cycle

precipitation
falls as rain, snow, or hail

condensation
water vapor cools as it rises

collection
becomes salt water, freshwater, or groundwater

evaporation
heat creates water vapor

19

Coming Back Up

Gravity moves water down, but many things bring it back up. Water can be brought up to the surface by tree roots. People can dig wells to reach it, too. This helps keep the water cycle moving!

GLOSSARY

absorb: to take in

atmosphere: the mix of gases around a planet

collect: to bring together

gravity: the force that pulls objects toward Earth's center

saturation: the state of being so full that nothing more can be added

surface: the top or outside of something

FOR MORE INFORMATION

BOOKS

Hammersmith, Craig. *The Water Cycle*. Mankato, MN: Capstone Press, 2012.

Kalman, Bobbie. *The Water Cycle*. New York, NY: Crabtree Publishing, 2006.

WEBSITES

The Water Cycle
kidzone.ws/water/
Find out just how old water is at this KidZone Science site.

The Water Cycle
studyjams.scholastic.com/studyjams/jams/science/ecosystems/water-cycle.htm
Learn all about the water cycle on this StudyJams site.

The Water Cycle
water.usgs.gov/edu/watercycle.html
Find out where Earth's water is found on this page.

Publisher's note to educators and parents: Our editors have carefully reviewed these websites to ensure that they are suitable for students. Many websites change frequently, however, and we cannot guarantee that a site's future contents will continue to meet our high standards of quality and educational value. Be advised that students should be closely supervised whenever they access the Internet.

INDEX